Usborne History of E

THE
FIRST
WORLD WAR

Usborne Quicklinks

The Usborne Quicklinks website is packed with thousands of links to all the best websites on the internet. The websites include information, video clips, sounds, games and animations that support and enhance the information in Usborne internet-linked books.

To visit the recommended websites for this book, go to the Usborne Quicklinks website at **www.usborne.com/quicklinks** and enter the keywords **The First World War**.

When using the internet please follow the internet safety guidelines displayed on the Usborne Quicklinks website. The recommended websites in Usborne Quicklinks are regularly reviewed and updated, but Usborne Publishing Ltd. is not responsible for the content or availability of any website other than its own. We recommend that children are supervised while using the internet.

USBORNE HISTORY OF BRITAIN

THE FIRST WORLD WAR

Henry Brook, Rob Lloyd Jones & Conrad Mason

Illustrated by Ian McNee

Designed by Anna Gould, Tom Lalonde & Stephen Moncrieff

Edited by Ruth Brocklehurst & Jane Chisholm

Consultant: Terry Charman, Imperial War Museum

Contents

Britain goes to war

At the start of the 20th century, Britain appeared to be at the peak of its powers, with its vast empire and booming industries. But all that was about to change, in a war that would destroy nations and cost millions of lives.

The First World War began in Europe, but its destructive power touched every corner of the globe. Britain won the war, but few people today celebrate it as a glorious victory. The British public were left stunned by years of slaughter in the battlefields, and the horrors of the war have had a lasting impact ever since.

Scott was beaten to the Pole and died with his friends only a few miles from safety. But their stamina and courage on the desperate journey across the ice struck a chord with the British public, and the explorers became national heroes.

Newspaper writers and poets claimed that Scott had given his life for the glory of his country. Even though he had failed in his mission, they saw Scott and his team as an example for young British people.

The same young men who were inspired by Scott's death would soon be signing up to fight and give up their own lives for their country.

Clash of empires

At the start of the 20th century, the British people were in a confident mood. Their empire was defended by the largest navy in the world, and their factories, cities and shipyards were thriving. It seemed as if they were entering a golden age of boundless wealth and global influence. But other nations were growing strong too, and governments across Europe were beginning to jostle for power and land.

Kaiser Wilhelm II of Germany was a cause of much concern. Not only were German industries beginning to overtake British ones, but the Kaiser was eager to build up his overseas empire and have a greater say in world affairs. He had been steadily expanding his armed forces and building a new fleet of warships. Some British observers worried that he was preparing for war.

Crewmen pull up the anchor of the *HMS Dreadnought* in October, 1906.

Taking sides

In the late 19th century European leaders made alliances and military agreements with other countries, forming two rival groups of powers. Austria-Hungary and Italy sided with Germany to form the Central Powers, while France, Russia and Britain joined together to form another group, the Triple Entente, which would later become known as the Allies.

This tangled web of pacts and promises – some of them secret – would make it difficult for any European country to stay out of future conflicts.

Arms race

In 1906, the British Royal Navy launched a fearsome new battleship called *HMS Dreadnought*. It was bigger, faster and had more firepower than any previous warship and gave its name to a new style of fighting ships – the dreadnoughts.

Kaiser Wilhelm was envious of the British fleet, and the Germans were soon building their own dreadnoughts. A fierce naval race started between the two countries, as both sides paraded their towering battleships around the ports of the world.

By 1914, the Royal Navy had 30 dreadnoughts and the Germans had 20. But while Britain and Germany competed for mastery of the seas, other governments were also modernizing their armed forces and drawing up detailed military plans for any attack. Relations between Europe's leaders became increasingly strained, as they listened for the distant drums of war.

A family affair

Most of the ruling dynasties across Europe were closely related through family ties to Britain's Queen Victoria. Nicknamed the Grandmama of Europe, three of the main figures in the First World War were her grandsons:

Britain's King George V

Tsar Nicholas II of Russia

The German Kaiser, Wilhelm II

Queen Victoria had taken the German family name, Saxe-Coburg-Gotha on her marriage to the German Prince Albert.

In 1917, anti-German riots and demonstrations took place in Britain, and George V changed this name to Windsor.

Sarajevo police seize one of the men involved in the assassination of Archduke Franz Ferdinand.

The spark

Princip was 19 when he was arrested. He received a 20-year sentence, but he was already suffering from tuberculosis, which eventually killed him. He died in prison on April 28, 1918.

On Sunday, June 28, 1914, gun shots rang out in the Bosnian capital of Sarajevo, and Europe slid closer towards war. The man who pulled the trigger was Gavrilo Princip, a member of a Serbian terrorist group. He shot and killed the heir to the Austro-Hungarian throne, Archduke Franz Ferdinand, sparking a chain of events that would drag Britain into the most destructive war the world had ever seen.

When the Austro-Hungarian government declared war on Serbia, Europe became divided. Germany backed Austria-Hungary, while the Russians supported the Serbs. On August 1, Germany declared war on Russia. When the French rallied their troops in support of the Russians, Germany declared war on them too.

Taking sides

This map shows the European alliances during the First World War.

- ░ Allies
- █ Central Powers
- ░ Neutral countries

1. MONTENEGRO
2. ALBANIA
3. GREECE
4. TURKISH EMPIRE

UNITED KINGDOM

BELGIUM

GERMANY

RUSSIA

FRANCE

AUSTRIA-HUNGARY

ITALY

BOSNIA

SERBIA

RUMANIA

BULGARIA

PORTUGAL

1.

2.

3.

4.

The two fronts

The Germans now faced fighting on two fronts – against France in the west and Russia to the east. They believed it would take the Russian army six weeks to muster their troops, so they hoped to crush France first, then turn their attention to the east. This was known as the Schlieffen Plan. Kaiser Wilhelm was so confident, he declared he would have "Paris for lunch, St. Petersburg for dinner". On August 4, the German army invaded Belgium, heading for Paris by the shortest, flattest route.

Britain's ultimatum

By invading Belgium, Germany had forced Britain's hand. Britain was bound by treaty to protect Belgium, whose ports provided a vital link to the rest of Europe. On August 4, the British government issued an ultimatum to Germany: withdraw from Belgium by midnight, or Britain would act. Midnight came, and there was no reply. Britain declared war on Germany.

The big guns

To speed their advance through Belgium, the Germans brought out a powerful secret weapon – a new type of siege cannon, known as Big Bertha.

These massive guns blasted Belgian forts from over 15km (9 miles) away. They marked the start of a new kind of warfare – a battle of machines as well as men.

New recruits like these in the Lincolnshire regiment learned basic rifle skills before being sent to fight.

Your country needs you

Most people in Britain believed their country would win a quick and decisive victory in the war. Street parties were held to celebrate, and huge crowds gathered in London to show their support. They thought the war would be over by Christmas.

But not everyone was so sure. Field Marshal Lord Kitchener, the Secretary of State for War, feared a long war that would drain Britain to its "last million men". The Germans had five million men ready to fight, while Britain's 200,000-strong army was tiny in comparison. Kitchener called for volunteers to join his 'New Army'.

"Goodbye Dolly I must leave you, though it breaks my heart to go, something tells me I am needed at the front to fight the foe..."

This popular song, called *Goodbye Dolly Gray*, was written before the war. It became popular again in 1914, as men enlisted for the British army.

Go! Fight!

Kitchener knew men would be more likely to enlist if they could fight alongside their friends, so he set up 'Pals Battalions' – groups of men from the same city, village or workplace who trained and fought together. At the same time, propaganda posters were put up across Britain, designed to build public enthusiasm for the war, and encourage young men to volunteer.

Signing up

Charged with patriotic fever, over 750,000 young men signed up in less than a month. Queues outside some recruitment offices stretched over a mile.

The minimum age for volunteers was eighteen, but boys as young as thirteen gave false names so they too could join up. Most were more worried about telling their mothers than they were about the dangers of battle. They saw the war as a grand adventure away from home.

Kitchener

Field Marshal Lord Herbert Horatio Kitchener was already a national hero, having led the army to several victories in earlier wars. Even so, some politicians saw him as a relic of an earlier age, unable to lead Britain in a modern war.

Kitchener was killed in 1916, when his ship struck a mine laid by a German submarine. His death was a huge blow to public morale.

Posters like this were plastered all over the country, encouraging men to join the army.

Field Marshal Lord Kitchener's distinctive face appeared on posters like this across Britain, urging young men to sign up.

BRITONS

"WANTS YOU"

JOIN YOUR COUNTRY'S ARMY!
GOD SAVE THE KING

Reproduced by permission of LONDON OPINION

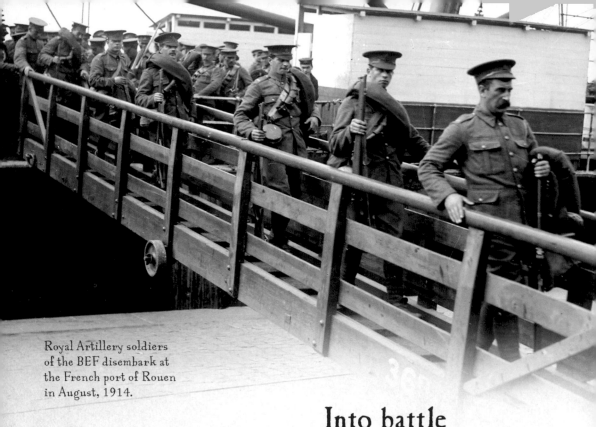

Royal Artillery soldiers of the BEF disembark at the French port of Rouen in August, 1914.

Into battle

Tommies

The men of the British Expeditionary Force were also nicknamed Tommies, from the name Tommy Atkins.

Atkins was the name used on military sample forms, but some people think Tommy Atkins had also been a heroic soldier in the 1800s.

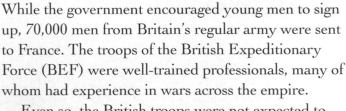

While the government encouraged young men to sign up, 70,000 men from Britain's regular army were sent to France. The troops of the British Expeditionary Force (BEF) were well-trained professionals, many of whom had experience in wars across the empire.

Even so, the British troops were not expected to play a major part in halting the German advance. Under the command of Field Marshal Sir John French, their orders were simply to support the much larger French army, while Britain's main contribution would come from its powerful navy.

The Kaiser was unimpressed by the small British army. He supposedly urged his troops to "walk over General French's contemptible little Army." This was probably just British propaganda, but it delighted the BEF. They landed in France in early August, proudly calling themselves the 'Contemptibles'.

Help from the colonies

Britain's colonies abroad also began recruiting troops for the war. Australia and New Zealand announced they would raise an army, and Canada offered 22,000 men, with a promise of half a million more by 1916. Even tiny Newfoundland declared itself ready to help Britain, "in every possible way."

But the most immediate contribution came from India, whose 160,000-strong army of well-trained troops was quickly mobilized. The war was taking place a long way from most of the colonies, but their people were proud to belong to the empire, and determined to help defend it.

"Our duty is quite clear – to gird up our loins and remember that we are Britons."

This declaration, by the Australian Prime Minister in August 1914, summed up the mood of many of Britain's colonies on the outbreak of war.

First contact

As the BEF made their way towards Belgium, Field Marshal French had received intelligence that the German army was marching towards the Belgian mining town of Mons. He had no idea of the size of the approaching army, but was convinced his men could halt their advance. They spread themselves along a 40km (25 mile) stretch of the Mons Canal, digging defensive trenches, and turning rickety mining huts into makeshift fortresses. Then they sat in wait.

By the morning of August 23, the German army – 90,000 strong – was upon them. The British put up stubborn resistance from across the canal, firing their rifles at such speed that the enemy thought they were facing machine guns. But by the afternoon the Germans had crossed the canal. Outflanked and outnumbered, French ordered his men to fall back.

The 'Contemptibles' had proved they wouldn't be beaten easily. But they were now in retreat, while the German advance continued.

Angel of Mons

Soon after the Battle of Mons, stories buzzed through the British troops of angels storming from the sky, protecting their soldiers with flaming arrows.

The myth began as a story in a newspaper, but many people believed it was true. The government was happy to let them; inspired by stories of Mons, thousands more British men signed up to fight.

French taxis gather in Paris. Around 600 taxis like these carried almost 6,000 reserve soldiers to the front.

Field Marshal French

Field Marshal Sir John French fought in several wars before taking command of the BEF.

He was shocked at how many of his men were killed in the early part of the war, and tried to avoid putting them in danger. In 1915 he was replaced by Douglas Haig, who was ready to sacrifice men if needed.

Saving Paris

With the Allies in retreat across northern France, German forces were tantalizingly close to their goal: Paris. Confident of victory, they advanced quickly, but they faced a final challenge on the outskirts of the city. French and British troops launched a fierce counter-attack, in a desperate effort to stop the Germans.

Last reserves

While the citizens of Paris prepared for disaster, French commanders mustered every available soldier to defend the capital. Using fleets of taxis to ferry reinforcements to the battlefield, they stopped the Germans in their tracks, only 50km (30 miles) from the city limits.

When French and British troops forced a gap in the enemy line at the River Marne, the Germans retreated to a ridge of high ground. Exhausted and short of supplies, they dug trenches to protect their territorial gains. Paris had been saved.

The Race to the Sea

Keeping up the attack, the Allies tried to rush their soldiers around the northern edge of the battlefield, in an attempt to threaten the enemy from the rear. But the Germans had the same idea. Both sides scrambled frantically north, digging trenches along the way to defend their positions.

This Race to the Sea, as it became known, ended in a dead heat in the sand dunes by the North Sea. Behind them lay hundreds of miles of trenches, snaking their way from the Channel coast to the borders of neutral Switzerland.

A new front

In October, the Germans attacked British forces in the Belgian region of Flanders, hoping to break through at the city of Ypres and capture the Channel ports. The soldiers of the BEF stood firm – but at the cost of tens of thousands of dead and wounded.

These losses broke the back of Britain's old, professional army and they were a taste of the carnage to come. Fighting rumbled on at Ypres until the winter weather arrived and soldiers dug in along a new battle line between the warring nations. This became known as the Western Front.

Battle lines

This map shows the sites of some of the key battles fought along the Western Front.

1. Mons (Aug. 1914)
2. Marne (Sept. 1914)
3. First Ypres (Oct. 1914)
4. Second Ypres (April 1915)
5. Loos (Sept. 1915)
6. Verdun (Feb. 1916)
7. Somme (July 1916)
8. Third Ypres (July 1917)
9. Cambrai (Nov. 1917)
10. Second Marne (July 1918)

— Front line at the end of 1914

THE NETHERLANDS

Calais · Dunkirk

Boulogne · Ypres FLANDERS 8.

3, 4. BELGIUM

5. Mons 1.

River Somme 7. 9.

LUXEMBOURG

· Rouen

River Seine

10. 6.

PARIS · 2.

River Marne

FRANCE

Six feet under

Soldiers were wet, cold and caked with mud in the trenches. Thousands were crippled by trench foot – an infection caused by the constant damp underfoot.

These British troops are wrapped in scarves and furs to keep as warm and dry as possible.

When the war started, men scratched holes in the earth to protect themselves from exploding shells and bullets. But, as the rival armies of Europe massed along the Western Front, they used all their manpower and industrial might to build a vast maze of trenches and tunnels. Few soldiers could have imagined that they would be living and fighting below ground for years.

Soldiers laid planks – or duckboards – over the trench floor to keep their feet out of the mud.

Home from home

The diagram below shows a typical layout of trenches on the Western Front.

By the end of the war, there were over 32,200km (20,000 miles) of trenches.

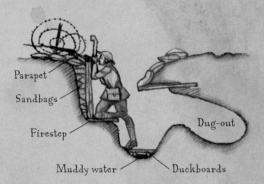

Parapet
Sandbags
Firestep
Dug-out
Muddy water
Duckboards

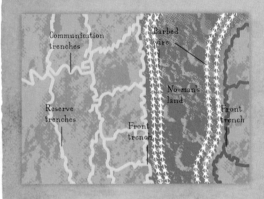

Communication trenches
Barbed wire
No-man's land
Reserve trenches
Front trench
Front trench

Soldiers peered into no-man's land over a parapet of sandbags, or curled up to sleep in dug-outs.

Some dug-outs were snug and dry, but most were just a hole in the dirt. Men put up signs naming them after luxurious places back home, such as Park Lane, Mayfair and the Ritz.

Heads down

Trenches were usually twisting and narrow, to make it harder for enemy raiders to rush through them. They were just deep enough to protect the average-sized man from any watching snipers, but thousands still died from head wounds.

The most dangerous times of day were at dawn and dusk, when the changing light made it difficult to spot attacks. Every man had to be on full alert, peering into the stretch of shell-scarred land that stretched to the enemy's front line. This ghostly strip of churned-up mud and tangled barbed wire was known as no-man's land. It was scattered with dead bodies, and crawled with rats and other vermin attracted to the stench of the battlefield.

Most soldiers spent around eight days in the front trench before moving back to safer reserve areas for a week's rest and other duties.

Creature comforts

Soldiers in the trenches enjoyed some comforts. They received a daily tot of rum in harsh weather.

Letters and parcels from home arrived quickly, and men read newspapers and books in quiet moments.

Royal gifts

King George's daughter, Princess Mary, set up a Christmas fund for Britain's soldiers and sailors. People gave so generously that each man received a brass tin, crammed with chocolates or cigarettes.

The card enclosed read, "With best wishes for a happy Christmas and a victorious New Year!"

British and German soldiers meet in no-man's land, Christmas Day, 1914.

A Christmas truce

Five months into the war, British troops were huddled together on the Western Front, fighting for survival against enemy fire and a brutally cold winter. When letters and gifts arrived from home they remembered their loved ones and friends lost in battle.

As the sun rose on Christmas Day, an extraordinary thing happened. Thousands of men gathered in no-man's land to celebrate Christmas with a day of peace.

Music and lights

Late on Christmas Eve, British sentries had heard voices on the night air. When they listened carefully they realized that the Germans were singing carols. Peering over the parapet of their trenches, they saw lights in the darkness. German soldiers had decked tiny Christmas trees with candles and put out signboards proposing a temporary ceasefire the following morning.

A strange meeting

Many British soldiers were reluctant to trust the enemy, but at dawn on Christmas Day they spotted small groups of unarmed Germans clambering slowly out of their trenches. In several sections of the British line, soldiers laid down their guns and stepped forward to meet them. Their officers tried to stop them at first, but they soon joined the crowd of quiet, curious men in no-man's land. In one part of the line, British and German commanders shook hands and exchanged gifts as they agreed the terms of a truce.

When dusk came, the soldiers returned to their posts and their guns were soon firing again. Army leaders were furious when they heard about the ceasefire. They ordered their officers to be more aggressive, insisting that they shell no-man's land throughout the Christmas season.

The Christmas truce was never repeated in the bitter years of fighting that followed.

Making friends

The soldiers in no-man's land chatted and swapped gifts of tobacco, food and buttons that they tore from their uniforms.

Some of the men played soccer...

...and one German, who had been a barber before the war, offered Tommies free haircuts.

Both sides took advantage of the truce to collect their dead from the battlefield.

John Singer Sargent's painting *Gassed* shows British soldiers injured and blinded after a gas attack.

Gas masks

At first, soldiers had no real protection against gas attacks.

Some placed wet cotton pads over their mouths. The chlorine dissolved in the water, so the soldier didn't breathe it in.

Later in the war, soldiers were issued with 'small box respirators' that filtered out the poison and protected against most gases.

Deadly weapons

The First World War was fought on a vast scale, with scientists developing terrifying new weapons to kill and maim, and industries churning out weapons and ammunition. From explosive shells to clouds of poison gas, there were a thousand different ways to die.

Fighting for air

In April 1915, Allied soldiers at Ypres noticed a yellow-green mist drifting over their lines. The Germans had opened hundreds of canisters of deadly chlorine gas, defying an international treaty that banned the use of chemical weapons. French colonial troops panicked and fled when the gas filled their trenches, burning their eyes, throats and lungs. This left the way open for a German advance – but the gas soon rolled away and Canadian soldiers moved in to close the gap.

Within a few months the British army retaliated by using gas in their attacks. It was unreliable, often changing direction on the wind, but it struck terror in soldiers' hearts. After Ypres, men had to carry masks and breathing equipment at all times.

Steel rain

Artillery shells killed more men in the war than any other weapon. Hidden miles behind the front line, field guns fired a barrage of millions of shells into enemy trenches before big battles. One soldier compared the explosion of an artillery shell to the force of an express train slamming into the earth.

Take cover

Soldiers hurled exploding grenades and carried shotguns for close-quarter fighting. Some men even carried homemade clubs for hand-to-hand combat. The Germans were the first to develop portable flamethrowers – spurting jets of burning fuel – and the Allies soon copied them.

But shotguns and flamethrowers were no match for the newly invented machine guns, as they spat out hundreds of bullets every minute. A single machine gun could defend long sections of trench, cutting down attacking infantry. Europe's armies were trapped in a long, grim war.

Grenade!

Grenades had been used before the First World War, but in the confined space of the trenches, they were particularly deadly.

British soldiers used 'jam tin bombs' – exploding cans packed with shards of metal. Soldiers could make their own with old jam tins.

In 1915, the British army introduced the Mills bomb, which was much more reliable.

German grenades had a handle to make them easier to throw, and were known as stick grenades or 'potato mashers' because of their shape.

In this photograph from June 1916, British troops are using massive field guns, called howitzers, to pound the enemy front line with shells.

Wounded British soldiers drink tea at a dressing station in 1916.

Battle scars

High-explosive shells ripped bodies apart and tore off soldiers' limbs, but they also damaged minds. In the days before doctors understood a lot about stress and mental trauma, men with shattered nerves were sometimes accused of cowardice. They risked brutal military punishments if they refused to fight.

Back to Blighty

Many soldiers hoped for a light wound in battle. Injuries that won them a ticket home were called 'Blighty wounds' – Blighty was army slang for Britain.

The walking wounded

Artillery barrages could last for days in the trenches. Shells landed every few seconds, shaking the earth with a deafening roar. It was impossible to sleep, and many soldiers lived in fear that the next shell might blow them to bits.

Almost one in fifty British soldiers showed symptoms of 'shell shock' during the war. This

22

was the term for nervous collapse caused by the strain of trench fighting. Shell shock affected people in different ways. Some men found it hard to think clearly and suffered from dizziness. Others couldn't stop shaking and were terrified by any sudden noise.

Army doctors thought soldiers with shell shock had brain damage, caused by the blast from exploding bombs. Most soldiers rested in hospital for a few days and then returned to the trenches, but others never recovered. They lived with the hidden scars of war for the rest of their lives.

Keeping order

Thousands of men tried to escape from the daily horrors of the front line by shooting themselves in the foot or the hand. But army doctors were ordered to watch out for these self-inflicted wounds, and if a man was found out he could easily be imprisoned or even shot. More than 300 British soldiers were executed after military trials – for cowardice, self-wounding and other serious crimes.

Broken on the wheel

But even Tommies who were guilty of minor crimes could suffer the dreaded Field Punishment No.1. They were bound, hand and foot, to the wheels of huge field guns or wooden posts.

This humiliating punishment lasted for several hours each day, and could go on for weeks. When they were cut down, there was no time to rest. They had to drill on the parade ground carrying heavy packs, surviving on a diet of bread and water.

Nursing the wounded

Women volunteers helped the injured and broken soldiers on the battlefields of the Western Front.

They drove field ambulances and worked as nurses in hospital tents behind the lines.

Often shelled and in danger, they always put the lives of others first.

One British nurse, Edith Cavell, hid wounded Allied soldiers in her hospital in Brussels, which was occupied by the Germans, and helped them to escape back home.

She was caught, and paid for her bravery with her life in front of a German firing squad.

On the Home Front

State control

The Defence of the Realm Act banned all sorts of activities:

NO GOSSIPING
about the army in public places.

NO FLYING KITES
or LIGHTING BONFIRES
– both of which could attract enemy airships.

NO FEEDING BREAD
to horses and chickens – it's a waste of food.

Away from the battlefield, the war had a huge impact on civilians' lives at home. Soon after the war broke out, Parliament passed the Defence of the Realm Act. This gave the government new powers to protect the country, and to control many aspects of daily life — it even limited how much alcohol people could buy, in an attempt to keep the nation's workforce sober.

War on words

The new act also helped the government to control information about the war. It became illegal for members of the public to write anything that might be useful to the enemy, or critical of the war effort.

Newspaper reporters were banned from the Western Front. At first, only one official correspondent was allowed to report on the war, although others were later given permission. Even then, the government had to approve everything they published.

Bored Germans play skittles to pass the time at Knockaloe on the Isle of Man. Like all Germans and Austro-Hungarians who were living in Britain when war broke out, they were held in detainment camps throughout the war.

Defending the realm

As part of the government's efforts to keep Britain safe from attack, the Royal Navy used its ships to set up a blockade in the North Sea. No enemy ship was allowed to get through, and all merchant vessels heading to Germany were stopped and had their cargos confiscated. In this way, naval commanders hoped to starve the enemy into surrender.

Home under fire

The British public had always trusted their mighty navy to keep them safe from German attacks. But in December 1914 German ships managed to get past the blockade, and shelled the coastal towns of Scarborough, Whitby and Hartlepool. The attack left 137 people dead, and many more wounded.

Just a month later, two huge German airships, known as zeppelins, appeared over the east coast of England. Bombs fell from them, killing four people below. It was the first of over fifty air raids over Britain that year, including several on London.

For the first time in centuries, British civilians were under direct attack, and home had become another front in the fighting. This was 'total war' – both civilians and soldiers were now involved in the battle to survive and defeat the enemy.

Airships, like this one, cruised at high altitudes, but they were still easy targets for planes and anti-aircraft guns on the ground. Several were shot down over Britain.

The Germans also used planes to launch bombing raids on Britain. This government poster shows people how to tell the difference between British and German aircraft and warns them to take shelter if they spot an enemy plane.

25

Women roll up their sleeves for some heavy work in Coventry in 1917.

White feathers

At the outbreak of the war, Admiral Charles Fitzgerald encouraged women to hand out white feathers to men who weren't in uniform. This was a traditional symbol of cowardice, and he hoped it would shame more men into joining the army.

Women mobilize

With more and more men fighting on the Western Front, it wasn't long before there was a shortage of workers to produce food and equipment. To solve this, everyone on the Home Front had to pitch in to help out with the war effort. Millions of women stepped into all kinds of jobs previously only done by men.

Until then, British women were usually expected to stay at home and look after the family. They didn't have as many rights as men, and weren't allowed to vote in elections or take any part in running the nation.

Women had been campaigning for the right to vote since Victorian times, and since 1903 a group, known as the suffragettes, had been fighting hard. They chained themselves to railings in public places, set fire to buildings, set off bombs and cut telegraph wires. But as Britain went to war, the suffragettes' leader, Emmeline Pankhurst, declared a truce, and called for the suffragettes to support the British war effort.

The shell scandal

In May 1915, British commanders complained that they were running short of shells and that many were 'duds' that failed to explode. The 'shell scandal' – as it became known – caused the government to rethink how it could produce lots of good quality ammunition.

The Liberal politician David Lloyd George was put in charge of solving the problem. He decided to enlist thousands of women to work in factories. These women – who became known as 'munitionettes' – worked long hours, handling dangerous chemicals and explosives. But they soon improved the quality and quantity of munitions sent to the front.

Hostility

Many trades unions, who represented workers' rights, resisted women taking men's jobs. They worried that women would accept less pay, and prevent men from working. So Lloyd George had to promise that, once the war was over, women would give up their jobs to make way for the returning soldiers. Despite this, many men remained hostile to the women workers. However, Lloyd George proved to be a capable and popular leader, and became Prime Minister in 1916.

More jobs for women

As the war dragged on, women took on a wider variety of jobs – from train driving and policing to coal mining. In 1917, the Women's Auxiliary Army Corps was set up, which sent many women to France. There they replaced soldiers who were working behind the front line, doing administration, training and cooking, so that more men could go to the front.

Canaries

Munitionettes got the nickname 'canaries' because the chemicals in shells turned their skin yellow.

Hungry Britain

By 1917, Britain was running low on food. A Ministry of Food was set up to solve the problem, and women were encouraged to join the 'Women's Land Army' of volunteer farm workers, to help grow more food. In 1918, the government brought in food rationing.

NATIONAL SERVICE
WOMEN'S LAND ARMY

GOD SPEED THE PLOUGH
AND THE WOMAN WHO DRIVES IT

APPLY FOR ENROLMENT FORMS AT YOUR NEAREST POST OFFICE OR
EMPLOYMENT EXCHANGE

Ambitious young
Winston Churchill had
been looking to make a
name for himself by
planning the
Dardanelles
campaign.
He was
forced to
resign
even before
the operation was over,
but later found the
success he craved as
Prime Minister during
the Second World War.

The Gallipoli Peninsula,
in northern Turkey

Black Sea

Constantinople
(now Istanbul)

Gallipoli
Peninsula

Dardanelles
Straits

TURKISH
EMPIRE

Aegean Sea

Bayonets at the ready,
Anzac troops scramble
uphill to attack the
Turkish front line.

Tackling the Turks

Even as the British government called for more men to
fill the trenches of the Western Front, vital troops were
being diverted beyond Europe to join the battle against
Germany's ally, the Turkish Empire.

Early in the war, the Turks had trapped Russia's
navy in the Black Sea by blocking off the Dardanelles
Straits, a narrow channel that provided Russia's only
link to the Mediterranean. Even so, Winston
Churchill, the young First Lord of the Admiralty, was
convinced the Royal Navy could find a way through.
As well as freeing the Russian fleet, he hoped the navy
could push on to the Turkish capital, Constantinople,
forcing the Turks to surrender.

A bad start

On 16 March, 1915, 16 British and French battleships
thrust into the narrow straits. The operation was a
disaster. Two British ships struck mines and sank,
while others were bombarded by shells from forts along
the cliffs of the Gallipoli Peninsula. Minesweepers were
sent in, but they quickly came under attack too. The
Allies had two options: retreat, or send land forces to
invade Gallipoli. The invasion was ordered.

Misery in Gallipoli

On April 25, 17,000 soldiers from the Australian and New Zealand Army Corps (Anzacs) joined British and French troops in an attack on the Gallipoli coast. Before the men had even climbed from their boats, Turks opened fire from trenches in the high ridges above the coves. Thousands of soldiers died before even reaching the shore. The sea was said to have run red with their blood. Unable to advance inland, they dug in for nine terrible months of trench warfare.

Sitting it out

Spring turned to summer, and the heat at Gallipoli became unbearable. Flies contaminated the soldiers' food, spreading disease. Then winter set in, with men suffering from both frostbite and pneumonia.

In November, the Allies finally admitted defeat and began the long task of withdrawing their troops from the peninsula. They had lost nearly 50,000 men, and had very little to show for it.

The man with the donkey

Among the Anzac heroes of Gallipoli were Australian soldier John Simpson Kirkpatrick, and his donkey Murphy. Each day, Kirkpatrick rode Murphy around hills dotted with enemy snipers, searching for wounded troops to carry back to the army hospital.

Kirkpatrick rescued over 300 men, before he was killed by a sniper. No one knows what happened to Murphy.

General Charles Townsend leads his troops through sandy Mesopotamia.

The wider war

Soldiers vitally needed on the Western Front were not only being diverted to the Middle East, but also to conquer German colonies beyond Europe. In 1914, 8,000 Indian troops were sent to invade German East Africa.

After a sweaty march through dense jungle, they were ambushed and defeated by German troops. At one point, the fighting roused an angry swarm of bees, forcing both sides to flee. Later, it became known as the Battle of the Bees.

Under siege

The defeat at Gallipoli came as a huge blow to British pride. Desperate for a morale-boosting victory against the Turks, military leaders turned their attention to the Middle East, where the Turkish Empire stretched beyond Jerusalem to the south and Mesopotamia (now Iraq) to the east. British and Indian troops had been stationed in Mesopotamia since before the war, guarding oil supplies in the Persian Gulf. Now they were ordered to advance north to capture the regional capital, Baghdad.

Led by General Charles Townsend, over 9,000 Indian and British troops advanced north, up the River Tigris. As they approached Baghdad on November 22, 1915, Turks attacked along the riverbanks. Townsend's men put up fierce resistance, but were forced to retreat, dragging over 4,000 wounded men to the dusty town of Kut-al-Amara. Turks immediately surrounded the town walls, cutting off their supplies. The Allies were trapped.

Trapped!

Barricaded behind the town walls, the men in Kut struggled through a terrifying 147-day siege – ravaged by enemy shells, weakened by freezing winter rains, and tortured by a desperate lack of food. Several attempts were made to rescue the besieged soldiers, but each was driven back by a Turkish force now bolstered by troops freed from Gallipoli. Meanwhile, conditions inside worsened. Diseases spread, and the food shortage became unbearable. Soldiers were dying in their dozens, starving to death within the city walls.

Out of the frying pan...

On April 29, 1916, Townsend finally surrendered. He had lost 1,750 men during the siege, but worse was still to come. Rounded up by brutal Turkish captors, the survivors were driven like cattle across the desert – whipped, beaten, and given little food or water. Over half the 8,000 soldiers who survived the siege died on the exhausting march to prison camps. It was another humiliating defeat at the hands of the Turks.

Besieged British soldiers guard against enemy planes on the walls of Kut-al-Amara.

Missing in action

Rudyard Kipling, one of the most popular writers in Britain, lost his 18-year-old son at Loos. Lieutenant John Kipling was listed as 'MIA' – missing in action.

Later in the war, Rudyard Kipling was given the task of writing an inscription to be carved on the graves of British soldiers. The inscription – 'Known unto God' – was carved onto a memorial, and later a gravestone, for his own son.

Stalemate

By the spring of 1915, Europe's armies were trapped in the mud. With no real breakthroughs on either side, the war had reached a stalemate. British generals struggled to find fresh tactics to break the deadlock, but they still had many lessons to learn.

A test of endurance

After the slaughter at Ypres, British military planners knew that when a soldier left the shelter of his trench he was an easy target for artillery gunners and snipers. Barbed wire, shell holes and ditches slowed down their advance, and commanders quickly lost contact with their superiors, making it hard to follow the progress of a battle. But most generals still thought that a massive infantry attack could overcome all obstacles.

In September 1915, the Allies launched a huge offensive against the Germans at Loos. In the battle that followed, the British released clouds of poison gas to drift over the German trenches, before tens of thousands of infantrymen stormed into no-man's land. But the gas turned on the wind, choking and burning the attackers. German machine guns scythed through the survivors and the British were beaten back to their trenches within days.

Firepower

Generals in the First World War had to adapt to a new, tactical problem. Although the design of military trenches had not changed for thousands of years, the weapons used to defend them had improved dramatically. With the invention of the automatic machine gun in the 1880s, groups of only a few trench soldiers could fight off thousands of troops.

To the last man

It would take years to develop the weapons, communications and tactics that would eventually unlock the Western Front. But at the end of 1915, British generals decided on a ruthless strategy for victory. It was called attrition. They would grind down the Germans with more shells, more troops and more attacks, until they were too exhausted to fight.

   But there would be a high price to pay in their war of attrition – the lives of millions of men.

This picture was taken by a British soldier. It shows British troops advancing through clouds of poison gas at the Battle of Loos.

The Eastern Front

In Eastern Europe, Britain's allies, the Russians, were locked in battle with the Central Powers along a vast battle zone that stretched from the Baltic coast down to the Black Sea. This line was known as the Eastern Front.

Partly because of its scale, fighting on the Eastern Front didn't become as bogged down in trenches as it did in the west. Instead, armies tried to outmanoeuvre each other and spring surprise attacks.

Despite suffering heavy casualties, the Russians had lots of men in reserve, and just sent more to the front.

Brave youth

Boy seaman John Cornwell was only 16 years old when he fought at the Battle of Jutland.

He was a member of a gun team onboard the HMS *Chester*. An explosion killed the rest of the team and wounded him, but he kept on fighting.

The ship returned safely to port and Cornwell was rushed to hospital. But he died the next day.

Cornwell was awarded the highest medal for bravery – the Victoria Cross – and the public turned out in droves for his funeral procession.

Ruling the waves

At the start of the war, the British had expected a huge naval battle with the Germans, which would settle once and for all who ruled the waves. But warships were extremely expensive to build, and neither side wanted to risk losing them in a big sea battle. So the Royal Navy preferred to maintain its blockade of Germany, while most of the German fleet was stuck in the North Sea, hemmed in by British ships.

Collision course

Then, in January 1916, the energetic Admiral Reinhard Scheer took charge of the German fleet. He thought his navy had been too timid, so he took the whole fleet out to sea, to hunt for British patrols.

British codebreakers picked up Scheer's radio messages, discovered his plans, and told Admiral John Jellicoe, who commanded the British fleet in the North Sea. Jellicoe decided to meet the Germans head on. He was taking a big risk – if the British lost control of the North Sea, they would be totally vulnerable. Winston Churchill described Jellicoe as, "the only man on either side who could lose the war in an afternoon."

The Battle of Jutland

On May 31, off Jutland in Denmark, the British and German fleets came face to face. Finally, it was the great naval engagement that both sides had been waiting for. Enemy ships pounded each other with shells, and thousands of men were killed by explosions or drowned in sinking ships. The fighting dragged on into the night, until finally Scheer turned his fleet and fled back to base.

The British had lost 15 ships, including three battle cruisers, while the Germans lost a single battle cruiser and 10 other ships. Scheer lost no time in claiming a victory for Germany. But the British had seen off the enemy fleet, and shown that they ruled the North Sea.

Danger underwater

After Jutland, there were no more big naval battles for the rest of the war. Instead, the Germans relied more and more on their submarines – known as U-boats – to slip past the British blockade and sink supply ships heading for Britain.

The U-boats sank many merchant ships, and succeeded in cutting down supplies to Britain. It was only in 1917 that the British managed to reduce their losses by having supply ships travel in groups, called convoys, protected by naval escorts.

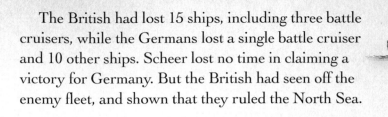

The Lusitania

In 1915, a U-boat sank a British passenger liner, the *Lusitania*, killing around 2,000 civilians, including more than 120 US citizens. This attack angered many Americans, who began to call for war on Germany.

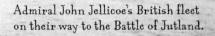

Admiral John Jellicoe's British fleet on their way to the Battle of Jutland.

This painting, from 1919, shows a battle in the sky between British and German aircraft. Some German pilots decorated their planes with bright paints. This led Allied pilots to nickname them the 'Flying Circus'.

Dogfights

Most air fights came down to one-on-one shootouts known as dogfights. Planes sometimes broke apart as the pilots dived and climbed, blasting each other with machine guns.

French and German pilots were equipped with parachutes, but British flyers weren't. Parachutes were considered too bulky, and some generals thought pilots would be tempted to jump at the first sign of danger.

Sky fighters

As the war continued at sea, British planes clashed with their enemies in the air. Early in the war, rival pilots that met in the sky had simply waved or taken pot shots at each other with their pistols. But designers soon realized that a plane fitted with machine guns could win battles in the air. Planes could also be used on spying missions above enemy positions, or even to launch bombing raids on enemy trenches.

Early fighter planes were not very effective. Machine gun bullets often hit their own aircraft's propellers, and bombs were released by the pilot, who simply tossed them over the side of his cockpit. But technology quickly developed, turning planes into agile fighters.

Throughout the winter of 1915, the Allies were losing two or three planes a day to superior German flyers. Allied casualties were so great, British pilots jokingly described their Royal Flying Corps (RFC) as the Suicide Club. But, as the war went on, the Allies improved their tactics, and won control of the skies.

Knights of the air

The most successful pilots of each nation became known as 'aces', and were presented as dashing daredevils in the popular press. The RFC's most successful ace was Major 'Mick' Mannock. He was almost blind in one eye, but he still managed to shoot down 73 German planes.

Victory in the sky

Early in 1917, new machines once again gave the Germans the upper hand. In April alone, the RFC lost 245 planes to German pilots. But, by the winter, the tide turned again, as German factories struggled to produce enough aircraft. New Allied planes, such as the British Sopwith Camel, combined power with agility, enabling the Allies to become the masters of the sky.

The Red Baron

The war's greatest flying ace was the German pilot Manfred Baron von Richtofen – better known as the Red Baron. Richtofen destroyed 80 Allied aircraft, before he was shot down and killed, in early 1918.

The Red Baron earned his nickname by painting his plane blood red. The sight of it approaching terrified inexperienced Allied pilots.

The Big Push

In the summer of 1916 the French army was fighting for its life at the Battle of Verdun. French commanders asked their allies to divert enemy troops and supplies from Verdun by launching a massive attack in the north, at the River Somme.

The new commander of the British forces, General Sir Douglas Haig, thought his army of young recruits would storm across the German line and advance for miles before the end of the first day. He believed that it would be 'The Big Push' that would win the war.

"The nation must be prepared to see heavy casualty lists."

Sir Douglas Haig made this grim statement shortly before the Battle of the Somme.

Haig was a gifted horseman and often went riding with his officers in the open country behind the lines.

Horsepower

Haig was an ambitious, stubborn man who had seen combat in Sudan and South Africa at the turn of the 20th century. He was a cavalry officer and, like many senior commanders, believed that horses had an important part to play in the war.

Although he later recognized the power of modern weapons, before the Somme Haig had described the machine gun as overrated. He mustered a large force of cavalry, ready to charge when his infantry cleared the enemy trenches.

A rain of fire

The battle began with a devastating British artillery barrage, lasting seven days and nights. Over a million shells hurtled across no-man's land and the thunder of the guns could be heard in London. For the soldiers crouching in the British trenches, it was a terrifying but reassuring noise. Their generals had promised the men that the barrage would kill all the German defenders hiding in their dugouts.

38

Troops of the 4th Battalion, the Worcestershire Regiment, march confidently on the way to the Battle of the Somme.

To add to the inferno above ground, engineers known as sappers exploded 21 mounds of high explosives, which they had hidden in long tunnels stretching beneath the enemy line.

The walk-in

As the dust settled from the explosions, the barrage stopped and whistles sounded on the morning air. Tens of thousands of British troops scrambled out of their trenches, while a smaller French army prepared to attack further south. It was 7:30am on July 1. The sun was already blazing as the British troops walked calmly across no-man's land.

Their officers had ordered them to advance slowly in long lines, to avoid any panic spreading through their ranks. Many of the soldiers had never been into battle before, but they strolled cheerfully across no-man's land to the broken German trenches, expecting an easy victory.

Shrinking soldiers

Early in the war, new recruits to the army were required to be at least 167cm (5ft 6 inches) tall.

But, as the war went on, the army became desperate for more men, and the limit was reduced. Special battalions were even formed for shorter men.

By February, 1916, height no longer mattered. Now, all fit single men aged 18 to 41 were conscripted – made to join the army.

The worst day

While the British calmly crossed no-man's land, thousands of German troops spilled out from underground bunkers, dragging machine guns, grenades and boxes of ammunition up to their trench positions. They had sat through the barrage in deep dugouts, safe from even the largest shells. It only took a few minutes to get their machine guns firing. Then the British troops heard the air hissing around them as bullets ripped through their lines.

Steel thorns

As the British struggled closer to the German trenches, they saw thick fields of barbed wire blocking their path. Instead of cutting the wire, the barrage had lifted it into the air and dropped it down in a tangled, impenetrable mess. Thousands of men were killed as they tried to hack their way through. Although the attack had already failed, new waves of British infantry were still leaving the trenches. Many of these soldiers were cut down before they could even step into no-man's land.

Landships

One of the most powerful symbols of modern warfare is the tank, which crushes everything in its path.

It was secretly developed by the British in 1915. While they were testing it, they called their new invention a 'water tank' to trick enemy spies. The tank name stuck.

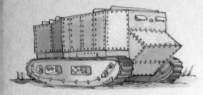

Although tanks offered a solution to the deadlock of trench fighting, early tanks broke down and got stuck too often to be effective weapons.

The British used 36 tanks at the Somme, but their first major success in battle was at Cambrai, in November 1917.

Counting the cost

When night fell, around 20,000 British soldiers were dead and thousands more were injured or missing. It was the bloodiest day in the whole history of the army, and has become a byword for the terrible slaughter of the First World War.

Many of the new Pals Battalions saw their first action at the Somme and they suffered heavy casualties. Hundreds of local communities across Britain lost almost all their men at a single stroke.

Haig kept his army in the field until November, when gales and lashing rain made fighting impossible. The British had gained a few miles of muddy ground and over a million German and Allied soldiers were dead and wounded.

British infantrymen advance through the barbed wire into no-man's land. This photograph is a still taken from the *Battle of the Somme*, a movie made in 1916 combining real footage of the battle with re-enactment scenes.

Divided loyalties

Thousands of soldiers from Irish regiments fought bravely on the first day of the Somme, but many had mixed feelings about British rule in Ireland.

Irish nationalists had been calling for independence from Britain long before the war, but when the fighting started they delayed their demands.

But as the war dragged on, some rebels grew frustrated. Two months before the Somme, they tried to seize Dublin and end British rule. The Easter Rising, as it became known, failed. Over a dozen rebel leaders were executed.

Forgotten heroes

Among the chaos of life on the front line, wounded or depressed troops often found comfort in the animals that scuttled around their trenches. Soldiers fed mice and birds that visited their dugouts, or kept spiders in matchboxes as pets. But animals were also put to work on the Western Front, often in terrible conditions.

In 1943, a British animal charity created a special award for animals that show incredible bravery in battle. So far, the PDSA Dickin Medal has been presented to 32 pigeons, 26 dogs, 3 horses and one cat.

War horses

As soon as war was declared, farmers across the country were asked to donate their horses to the war effort. The army expected them to be used in battle. But horses were useless among the barbed wire and bullets of trench warfare, so instead they were put to work hauling heavy supplies around the front line.

Horses suffered terribly – from exhaustion, disease and starvation. During the course of the war, eight million died, and two and a half million were injured. The British army's Veterinary Corps cared for the wounded beasts. But as soon as the animals recovered, they were sent back to work.

"I had the terrible experience to see three horses and six men disappear under the mud. It was a sight to live in my memory. I can still recall the cries of the trapped soldiers... and the last horse going into a muddy grave."

A soldier recalls the terrible sight of horses drowning under the weight of their own loads in the summer of 1916.

Thousands of horses suffered like this on the Western Front – sinking into deep mud as they hauled heavy supplies.

Winged messengers

Animals were useful for their speed as well as strength. Amid the confusion of battle, radio communication was often impossible. Instead, the army released special pigeons, trained to fly back to base with messages attached to their legs. Over 100,000 carrier pigeons were used on the Western Front. Some flew over 2,500km (1,500 miles) on their vital missions.

A soldier's best friend

Dogs were busy on the front line too, racing from trench to trench with messages in their collars, or acting as guards against enemy patrols. Some were trained to work as ambulance dogs, delivering medical supplies, food and water to injured men stuck in no-man's land. As well as urgent supplies, these dogs brought much-needed comfort to soldiers that were trapped in the battlefield. It meant they knew they had not been forgotten.

Animals under fire

Soldiers tried to shoot enemy carrier pigeons to stop messages from getting through. But they were too fast even for riflemen. So, faster birds, such as hawks, were released to kill the messengers instead.

Dogs were targeted by enemy snipers too, as they snuck beyond the trenches to lay secret telegraph lines around no-man's land.

Carrying rolls of wire on their backs, the dogs crept through dangerous territory, laying the lines behind them as they went.

A war of words

The First World War was remarkable in that it was the first conflict in which most British soldiers could read and write. Officers recited rousing speeches from Shakespeare to their troops, and soldiers spent long hours curled up with books, or writing letters home. Letters helped them feel close to loved ones – their words would reach home, even if they never did.

Many soldiers also kept diaries of their lives in the trenches. They knew they were witnessing remarkable events in human history, and set out to record what they saw. Writing before the Battle of the Somme, British private James Beatson described a hellish existence of, "alternating rushes and rests, shrapnel and stink bombs, bursting and sickening us with poisonous fumes and inflaming our eyes."

Stirring words

At the time of the war, poetry was seen as an important way of expressing powerful beliefs. Talented young poet Rupert Brooke, who died on the way to Gallipoli, was fascinated by the idea of soldiers giving their lives for their country. His poem *The Soldier* captured the spirit of patriotic duty that gripped thousands of men enlisting to fight:

Writing home

By the end of the war, the Army Postal Service employed over 4,000 soldiers. Even soldiers at the front line could write and receive letters from home.

Junior officers were supposed to check the letters and remove any sensitive details about military tactics. Many officers, though, felt uncomfortable reading soldiers' private mail, so the letters reached home without being changed.

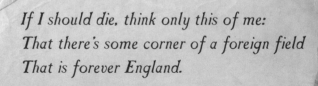

If I should die, think only this of me:
That there's some corner of a foreign field
That is forever England.

Hard truths

Faced with the grim reality of life in the trenches, later soldier poets mocked the idea of noble self-sacrifice. Writers like Wilfred Owen and Siegfried Sassoon had experienced battle first-hand. The heroes of their poems are brave but terrified men, fighting simply to stay alive. Owen's poem *Dulce et Decorum Est* takes its title from a Latin phrase meaning "it is sweet and right to die for your country". Owen calls this idea an "old lie" as he describes soldiers struggling in mud near the front line:

> *Bent double, like old beggars under sacks,*
> *Knock-kneed, coughing like hags, we cursed*
> *   through sludge...*

Siegfried Sassoon's poems, too, are filled with images of the horrors of battle. The soldiers he depicts are "dizzy with galloping fear" as shells batter their trenches. After the war, Sassoon became deeply concerned with the fate of soldiers who had, like himself, lived through these terrible events. His poem *Does it Matter?* urges readers not to forget their sacrifices:

> *Do they matter?–those dreams from the pit?...*
> *You can drink and forget and be glad,*
> *And people won't say that you're mad;*
> *For they'll know you've fought for your country*
> *And no one will worry a bit.*

Soldier poets like Sassoon became hugely popular in the years after the war. Their gritty, honest accounts were a stark contrast to the stirring government propaganda printed in newspapers back home. They opened people's eyes to the horror of war.

Siegfried Sassoon

Sassoon and Owen

In 1917, British officer Siegfried Sassoon wrote to a newspaper, calling the war unjust. The army claimed his nerves were shattered, and sent Sassoon to a military hospital. There, he met Wilfred Owen and the two became close friends.

Both poets hated war, but returned to the trenches, feeling it was their duty to write about what was happening.

After Owen died in 1918, Sassoon arranged for his friend's poems to be published. Today they are among the most famous words written about the war.

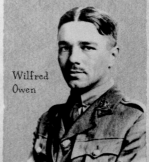

Wilfred Owen

This US army poster shows a globe, urging recruits to see the war in Europe as their problem too.

Secret Room 40

Secret German messages such as the Zimmerman Telegram were read by intercepting radio and telegram signals. The coded signals were then sent to Room 40 of the Admiralty Building in London, where they were deciphered by expert code breakers.

The code breakers included crossword champions, mathematicians, and language experts. Together they cracked over 15,000 vital German messages.

American allies

By early 1917, the Allied campaign was flagging. Food supplies were running low across Britain as German U-boats targeted the nation's supply ships. Mutinies rippled through the French army, and revolution in Russia would soon force the Russian army out of the war altogether. The Allies desperately needed help if they were to avoid defeat. They looked across the Atlantic to America.

Americans had so far distanced themselves from what they regarded as 'Europe's war'. But, as German submarines continued to attack non-military ships, American public opinion swung against the Central Powers. Worse, German agents now turned against America itself – sabotaging arms supplies destined for the Allies, and even planting a bomb in the US Capitol building in Washington. The Germans were convinced America would enter the war on the side of the Allies, so they resolved to treat the United States as an enemy.

The final straw...

Still, US President Woodrow Wilson remained hesitant to enter the war. Then, in January 1917, British agents in London intercepted a secret telegram from German foreign minister Arthur Zimmerman to his ambassador in Mexico City. It ordered him to form an alliance with Mexico and Japan against the United States. Zimmerman hoped that if the Americans faced conflict on their own doorstep, they would be too distracted to send troops to Europe.

But when details of Zimmerman's telegram broke in the newspapers, Americans were outraged. President Wilson was left with no choice – on April 6, 1917, the United States declared war on Germany.

Help is coming

The first soldiers of the American Expeditionary Force reached Europe in June 1917, parading through the streets of Paris to the delight of gathered crowds. The US army was only around 130,000 strong, but President Wilson had already called for more volunteers, promising to fight with, "force to the utmost, force without stint or limit." By the end of the war, around two million American soldiers had arrived in Europe, with the full backing of America's vast financial and industrial resources.

To exhausted British troops stuck on the Western Front, America's entry into the war came as a huge boost. They tied pamphlets to balloons announcing the news and released them over enemy lines. The British knew that the depleted German army was no match for the fighting power of their new ally.

It seemed that, finally, the stalemate in the trenches might be broken.

Mighty Marines

The best-trained American troops sent to France were an elite force called the Marines. US Marines fought so fiercely against the Germans that they earned the nickname Devil Dogs.

Cheering soldiers of the American Expeditionary Force pile onto a ship as they set sail for France.

Drowning in mud

While the Americans were raising an army to send to Europe, General Haig was determined to keep up pressure on the Germans. He believed that the enemy's strength and morale had been broken at the Somme, so he decided to break out of Ypres and seize the high ground around the village of Passchendaele. From there, his soldiers could attack and destroy the German navy's U-boat bases along the Belgian coast.

Rain and mud

In July, 1917, Haig prepared to launch the third Battle of Ypres. He ordered a ten-day barrage of the German front line, and then sent his troops into battle. But, instead of breaking the enemy line, the barrage had churned up all the fields around Passchendaele. Unusually heavy rain turned them into a nightmarish swamp of thick mud, broken roads and flooded shell holes.

A hollow victory

In these terrible conditions, the attack descended
into chaos. British supply vehicles couldn't cross
the treacherous quagmire, while artillery sank and
constantly had to be hauled out. Wooden tracks called
duckboards were laid down for the infantry to walk
across but, even so, thousands of men drowned in
the liquid mud of the battlefield. In spite of the huge
numbers of troops lost, Haig continued with the assault.

After months of terrible carnage, Canadian soldiers
finally occupied Passchendaele village in November.
It was a hollow victory. The Allies couldn't advance to
the U-boat bases, and German troops soon recaptured
all their lost ground. To many people, Passchendaele
became a symbol of warfare on the Western Front
– a terrible waste of life, for hardly any gain.

"I died in hell –
(They called it
Passchendaele)"

From Siegfried
Sassoon's poem
Memorial Tablet,
written from the
point of view of a
soldier who died at
Passchendaele.

In this photograph by Frank Hurley,
Australian soldiers walk across wooden
duckboards over the flooded battlefield of
Passchendaele. In many places, stepping off
the duckboards meant drowning in the mud.

War in the east

While Haig's army was bogged down in the mud of Passchendaele, British troops in the Middle East were finally enjoying some success against the Turks.

In June 1917, after the disaster at Gallipoli, and two failed attempts to capture the Turkish stronghold at Gaza in Palestine, a new commander had taken control of British troops in the region. His name was Sir Edmund Allenby, and he was determined to prove his worth by defeating the Turkish empire as quickly as possible.

Sir Edmund Allenby enters Jerusalem after the city's surrender.

Jerusalem by Christmas

Allenby was a brilliant commander. He soon captured Gaza, using heavy artillery to keep the enemy pinned in place, and sending cavalry sweeping around the sides to attack. Then he advanced on Jerusalem. Allenby was ordered to take the city by Christmas of 1917, but its governor surrendered on December 9 after just a day's fighting.

Defeating the Turks

Allenby's troops weren't the only ones putting pressure on the Turks. Many Arabs inside the Turkish empire wanted to be free from Turkish rule, and the British persuaded the Arab leader Sherif Hussein to lead a revolt. In the Arabian desert, Hussein's forces carried out guerrilla raids and sabotage, under the direction of a British officer, T. E. Lawrence. At the same time, another British force was attacking the Turkish army in Mesopotamia, advancing up the River Tigris to take Baghdad.

It was all too much for the Turks. When Allenby launched an assault near Megiddo in Palestine, in September 1918, their army crumbled. Soon after that, the Turkish government surrendered, and the war in the Middle East was over.

A broken promise

For the Arabs, though, the victory was no cause for celebration. In 1915, the British had promised them that they would get their own state after the war. But in the peace negotiations, the Allies divided up control of the Middle East among themselves. Many Arabs were furious with the British for going back on their word.

Lawrence of Arabia

T. E. Lawrence began the war serving as an intelligence officer in Cairo, before moving to fight with the Arabs.

Lawrence wanted to help the Arabs get their own state. Even after the war, he continued to argue on their behalf.

In 1935, he died in a motorcycle accident. He had become famous for his writing about the war, including his autobiography called *The Seven Pillars of Wisdom*. The 1962 film *Lawrence of Arabia* tells his story.

T. E. Lawrence often wore traditional Arab dress, to the annoyance of his superior officers.

Backs to the wall

As Allenby made progress in the Middle East, British troops on the Western Front were plunged into a desperate fight for survival.

On March 21, 1918, the German senior commander Erich Ludendorff launched the 'Spring Offensive' – a surprise attack, which aimed to defeat the Allies before US troops arrived in force.

Russian surrender

Just weeks before the Spring Offensive, the Russians signed a peace treaty with Germany. The Tsar's government had collapsed the previous year, and the new Russian leaders didn't want to carry on with the war.

This meant that many German troops who had previously been fighting the Russians on the Eastern Front were now free to take part in the offensive in the west.

Taken by storm

The assault began with a fearsome barrage on the weakest part of the British line, near the Somme. This was followed by a ground attack, led by 'storm troopers' – the cream of the German army. They were under orders to advance as fast as possible, while the rest of the army came behind, mopping up the remains of any British resistance.

British gunners fire a 60-pounder artillery piece at the advancing Germans, on the fifth day of the Spring Offensive.

Fighting back

Outnumbered, the British were rapidly forced back. Thousands were killed, and many more were taken prisoner. The Allied commanders held an emergency meeting. They agreed that the French General Ferdinand Foch would now take charge of all Allied forces, to coordinate the fight against the Germans.

Under Foch's command, reinforcements, artillery and supplies were brought in by train, and the British began to stand firm against the German attacks. Frustrated, Ludendorff moved his offensive to different parts of the Allied line, trying to break through wherever he could.

> "With our backs to the wall, and believing in the justice of our cause, each one of us must fight on to the end."
>
> On April 11, 1918, General Sir Douglas Haig sent a Special Order of the Day encouraging the British to fight to the death.

Last gasp

By July, the German attacks were faltering everywhere against the Allied lines. Both sides had lost hundreds of thousands of men, but the German casualties included many storm troopers – their very best soldiers.

Ludendorff's army had captured more territory than the Allies had managed in the war so far. But his troops were exhausted, and spread over a wide area, with no artillery support. They were also running low on supplies – guns, ammunition, and even food. The Royal Navy's blockade was as tight as ever, and now German factories didn't even have enough materials to make shells for the army.

In July 1918, the Germans launched their last assault, at the Second Battle of the Marne. But, supported by British tanks and by newly-arrived US troops, the Allies counter-attacked and forced the Germans into retreat. The Spring Offensive had failed.

Munitions war

British industry played an important part in stopping the Spring Offensive. British factories were making vast numbers of shells, guns and artillery pieces, which were sent to replace those that the Germans had captured or destroyed.

The Hundred Days

With more US troops arriving every day, the Allied commanders decided that it was time to turn the tables and strike back. So, on August 8, 1918, the British led a surprise attack on the German line at Amiens. It was the first blow in the offensive that would end the war – the 'Hundred Days' – from August 8 to November 11.

Amiens

The British used a new combination of tactics. Instead of a long bombardment before the attack, British gunners used new targeting techniques to fire a short, accurate barrage, destroying almost all the enemy guns before the battle had even started. Then the infantry advanced, with a fleet of tanks, protected by a 'creeping barrage' – a steady bombardment which 'crept' toward the enemy, just in front of the infantry.

    The tactics were a huge success. On the first day, the British stormed the German line, killing and capturing around three times as many men as they lost. After years of trench warfare, the tide had finally turned, and the Germans were pushed back. "They no longer have even a dim hope of victory on this Western Front," wrote the British reporter Philip Gibbs.

Bite and hold

Throughout August and September, the Allies pushed on, winning more and more ground. They advanced using a 'bite and hold' method. This meant attacking and advancing a short way, then waiting for the artillery to catch up. In this way they made slow, steady progress until they reached the Germans' so-called 'Hindenburg Line' in mid-September.

Colonial courage

Troops from British colonies – especially Canadians and Australians – were at the forefront of many battles during the Hundred Days offensive.

In fact, the offensive is sometimes called 'Canada's hundred days' in memory of the Canadians' efforts.

At the end of August, Australian troops attacked uphill and stormed the German stronghold at Mont St. Quentin.

The British General Henry Rawlinson described it as the greatest military achievement of the war.

Several Australian soldiers were awarded the Victoria Cross after the battle.

Breaking the line

The Hindenburg Line was a warren of trenches, barbed wire and concrete fortifications, up to 5km (three miles) wide in some places. When it was built in 1916, commanders on both sides believed that it was impenetrable. Now the Allies hoped that their new tactics would help them break through.

On September 26, massed British artillery began raining endless shells on the Hindenburg Line, while tanks and infantry attacked on the ground. The line crumbled. By October 5, the Germans were retreating all along the Western Front. Finally, the end of the war was in sight.

Spanish flu

To add to the Germans' woes, many of their soldiers were weakened or killed in late 1918 by the 'Spanish flu' – a deadly flu virus. The next year, the virus went on to kill millions worldwide.

Victorious British troops rest on the banks of the St. Quentin Canal. This was one of the best-defended parts of the Hindenburg Line.

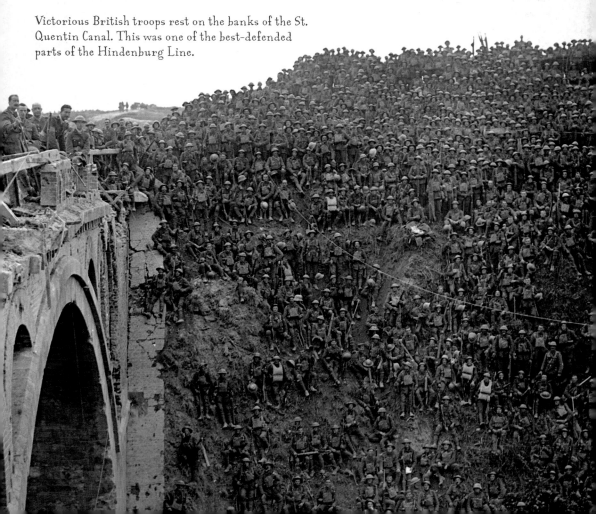

Peace at last

By November, Germany was on the brink of collapse.
There was a mutiny in the navy and riots in the streets,
and the Kaiser had to stand down and flee the country.
Germany's allies had already made peace. At last,
German leaders approached the Allies to do the same.

In the early morning of November 11, in a train
carriage in woods near the front line, German and
Allied leaders signed an armistice – an agreement to
stop fighting. And at 11am, the eleventh hour of the
eleventh day of the eleventh month, the guns fell silent.
The First World War was at an end.

Many British soldiers couldn't believe it was all over.
In some parts of the line, they even continued to fight
for hours after the war had ended. But, in Britain and
throughout its empire, celebrations were held.
Everyone was excited that the soldiers were
coming home at last.

Day to remember

When news of the peace
reached London, many
people sang and danced
in the street. Others rode
around the city on
double decker buses
covered in Union Jacks.

Here, Londoners hold
a children's tea party
in August 1919, to
celebrate the return
of peace. The street is
decorated with flags
and paper chains.

Make them pay

Meanwhile, Allied leaders prepared to meet and discuss how to keep the peace. On December 14, the public elected David Lloyd George to continue as their Prime Minister. He would represent Britain at the peace talks.

Like many British people, Lloyd George thought that the war was Germany's fault, and he wanted to make sure the Germans wouldn't be able to fight again. In his election campaign, he won a lot of support because he promised to, "make the Germans pay."

But it wasn't going to be easy. While the French Premier Georges Clemenceau wanted to punish Germany as much as possible, US President Wilson was more concerned with finding ways to keep the peace in the future.

Lloyd George, French Premier Clemenceau, and US President Wilson

Versailles

After months of negotiation, the Allies finally came up with a treaty that all three leaders were prepared to accept. It was signed on June 28, 1919, at the Palace of Versailles outside Paris.

The treaty forced the Germans to cut their armed forces and pay vast reparations (compensation money) to the Allied nations. There was also a 'war-guilt clause' which stated that Germany was to blame for starting the war. Most Germans thought the treaty was far too harsh. Many British people were dismayed too. The economist John Maynard Keynes walked out of the talks, predicting that the reparations would ruin Germany and lead to another war. Sadly, he was to be proved right.

Corporal Hitler

Among the Germans who were angry at the Treaty of Versailles was a young corporal named Adolf Hitler.

Hitler believed that the Germans at home had betrayed their soldiers, by making peace when the German army had not been totally defeated.

Just twenty years later, Hitler rose to become dictator of Germany, and launched a world war that would be even more bloody than the first.

The Allies had won the war, but when the parties that marked the Armistice were over, life couldn't simply go back to the way it was before 1914. Things would never be the same again.

Voting for change

Britain before the war had been a place of marked inequality, between rich and poor, and men and women. Not only were women excluded from taking part in elections, but men below a certain income weren't allowed to vote either. But during the war, the old social divisions began to break down as women took over men's jobs and men from all walks of life fought and suffered alongside one another in the trenches.

Many people believed British society should be made fairer. So in 1918, the government passed a law giving the vote to all men over 21 and all women over 30. After the 1918 General Election, Lady Nancy Astor became the first female MP to sit in Parliament.

The Irish question

In the same election, the Irish nationalist party, Sinn Féin, won 73 out of the 105 Irish seats in Parliament, but refused to take them up. Sinn Féin decided this was their chance to claim independence from the United Kingdom. They set up their own parliament, called the Dáil, and began organizing the Irish Republican Army (IRA) to drive the British out. Not everyone in Ireland wanted independence, so this sparked off a violent civil war.

Fit for heroes?

Lloyd George promised that British soldiers would return to a land fit for heroes to live in. But the reality was very different. Industries no longer needed to produce shells and equipment for war, and so there weren't enough jobs for the returning soldiers. Some even ended up begging on the streets.

One soldier, a machine gunner named George Coppard, later published his wartime diaries. Coppard describes how he was unable to find work after the war.

Meanwhile, high ranking officers received rewards of thousands of pounds. Haig was made an earl for his services in the war.

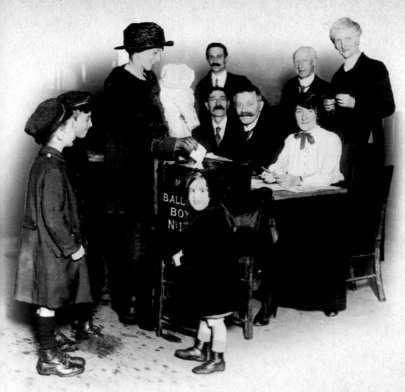

A woman casts her vote for the first time in the 1918 General Election.

In 1921, Sinn Féin and the British government reached an agreement. Northern Ireland remained part of the UK, and southern Ireland became independent. But the struggle for control of Ireland was far from over.

Empire in decline

The winds of change were blowing across Britain's wider empire too. Troops and money from the colonies had been vital to the war effort, and many emerged with a strong sense of national identity. In Australia and New Zealand, for example, people still proudly remember their war dead on 'Anzac day' – April 25 – every year.

Along with growing national pride, many people in the colonies, particularly in India, Australia and Canada, now pushed for more independence and the right to run their own affairs. The once-mighty British empire was finally in decline. In the wake of the First World War, it seemed as if the world had changed, forever.

Black and Tans

For some British soldiers, there was hardly any break from fighting after the war ended.

During 1919, the IRA attacked police and government buildings in Ireland, and the British government sent in war veterans to help keep order. They were known as 'Black and Tans' because at first, their uniforms were a mixture of dark police and tan army clothing.

Both the IRA and the Black and Tans won a reputation for terrible violence. Black and Tans often stopped people in the street and searched them at gunpoint.

59

Remembrance

> "Look up, and swear
> by the green of the
> spring that you'll
> never forget."

From *Aftermath*, by
Siegfried Sassoon

Tyne Cot military
cemetery, in Belgium,
is the largest of several
cemeteries built for
British soldiers who died
on the Western Front.

Around 900,000 soldiers from Britain and its empire
died in the First World War, and many more went
missing, or were terribly wounded. Long after the
fighting had ended, those soldiers who survived were
still unable to forget the horrors they had witnessed.

During the war, the Imperial (now Commonwealth)
War Graves Commission was set up to build and
maintain cemeteries near the battlefields. So that no
grave looked more important than another, each was
marked by a simple headstone recording a name
and a date.

Back in Britain, many communities, schools and workplaces set up their own war memorials, carved with the names of those who had died. In the years following the war, November 11, the anniversary of the Armistice, was set aside as a day of remembrance.

The greatest tragedy of the First World War was that it was not the 'war to end all wars' that everyone had thought it would be. Just 20 years later, the world would be plunged into another conflict, which would claim even more lives than the first.

Lest we forget...

Many soldiers were struck by the beauty of the poppies that grew on the battlefields after the fighting had stopped.

Later, the poppy became a symbol to remember those who had died.

Index

Acknowledgements

Every effort has been made to trace and acknowledge ownership of copyright. If any rights have been omitted, the publishers offer to rectify this in any future editions following notification. The publishers are grateful to the following individuals and organizations for their permission to reproduce material on the following pages: (t=top, b=bottom, m=middle, l=left, r=right)

Cover (t) IWM CO-874, **(bl)** Q1209, **(br)** COL-24.

p1 IWM 10470; **p2-3** The Art Archive/Imperial War Museum; **p6** The Naval Historic Center; **p8 (t)** © Bettmann/Corbis; **p10 (t)** The Art Archive/Imperial War Museum; **p11 (l)** The Art Archive/Imperial War Museum/Eileen Tweedy; **p11 (r)** The Art Archive/Imperial War Museum/Eileen Tweedy; **p12 (t)** © Roger-Viollet/Topfoto; **p14 (t)** © Bettmann/Corbis; **p16** IWM Q49104; **p18-19** IWM 35801; **p20 (t)** The Art Archive/Imperial War Museum; **p21(b)** The Art Archive/Imperial War Museum; **p22 (t)** IWM 4501; **p24 (b)** Courtesy of Manx National Heritage; **p25 (t)** IWM Q58481, **(mr)** © Hulton Archive/Getty Images; **p26 (t)** Hulton Archive/Getty Images; **p27 (b)** Library of Congress, Prints & Photographs Division, WWI Posters, [LC-USZC4-11192]; **p28-29** © Corbis; **p30 (t)** IWM 92658; **p31 (b)** IWM 197190; **p32-33** IWM HU 63277B; **p34 (tl)** IWM Q27025A; **p34-35** © akg-images; **p36-37** The Art Archive/Imperial War Museum; **p38 (bl)** © Bettmann/Corbis; **p39 (t)** IWM Q716; **p40-41** The Art Archive/Imperial War Museum; **p42 (tl)** Courtesy PDSA; **p42-43 (b)** IWM Q5943; **p44 (m)** Extract from the diary of Private James Beatson, by kind permission of Mrs. M. Robinson, **(bl)** *The Soldier* by Rupert Brooke, **(br)** IWM Q5242; **p45 (tr)** © Hulton-Deutsch Collection/Corbis, **(m)** *Dulce et Decorum Est* from Wilfred Owen: *The War Poems*, ed. Jon Stallworthy (London: Chatto & Windus, 1994), **(bl)** *Does It Matter?* by Siegfried Sasson, Copyright Siegfried Sassoon by kind permission of the Estate of George Sassoon, **(br)** The Art Archive; **p46 (tl)** The Art Archive/Eileen Tweedy; **p47 (mr)** Library of Congress, Prints & Photographs Division, WWI Posters, [LC-USZC4-7779], **(b)** © Corbis; **p48-49 (b)** IWM E(AUS)001220; **p50** IWM Q12616; **p51 (br)** Hulton Archive/Getty Images; **p52** The Art Archive/Imperial War Museum; **p55** IWM 9534; **p56** Topical Press Agency/Hulton Archive/Getty Images; **p57 (tr)** © Bettmann/Corbis; **p58 (bl)** Topical Press Agency/Hulton Archive/Getty Images; **p59 (t)** Popperfoto/Getty Images; **p60-61** © Michael St. Maur Sheil/Corbis.

Some of the photographs, both on the cover and inside this book, were originally in black and white and have been digitally tinted by Usborne Publishing. Some images have also been cropped for reasons of space.

For more information about the Imperial War Museum, go to **www.iwm.org.uk**

Additional illustrations by Dai Evans & Lynn Stone
Digital design by John Russell; Picture research by Ruth King